PORTRAIT SERIES

The RYE and CAMBER TRAMWAY

compiled by
Colin Judge

THE OAKWOOD PRESS

© Oakwood Press and Colin Judge 1995

British Library Cataloguing in Publication Data
A Record for this book is available from the British Library
ISBN 0 85361 473 3

Typeset by Oakwood Graphics

Printed by Alpha Print (Oxford) Ltd, Witney, Oxon

All rights reserved. No part of this book may be reproduced or transmitted in any form or by any means, electronic or mechanical, including photocopying, recording or by any information storage and retrieval system, without permission from the Publisher in writing.

Rye   The Ypres Tower.
The old Ypres Tower in Rye, once a jail and constructed in the reign of Edward III.
Author's Collection

Front Cover, above: A coloured commercial postcard by A.H. Homewood, Burgess Hill, Sussex and dated 12th August, 1904 shows the train passing Golf View. Passengers could request to alight here but no platform was provided and it was referred to as Halfway House. *Roger Kidner Collection*

Front Cover, below: Another view from a commercial postcard showing the petrol locomotive at Camber Sands *c.* 1931. *Colonel Stephens Railway Museum*

Rear Cover: A handbill advertising Easter services, believed to be for Easter 1939. The last year of operation. *Colonel Stephens Railway Museum*

Title Page: The 4wP 0-4-0 at Camber Sands with driver George Wratten. *Real Photographs*

Other books in this series
Railways of the Channel Islands - A Pictorial Survey *compiled by Colin Judge*
Glory of Electric Trams *by D.D. & J.M. Gladwin*
Peak Line: A Pictorial Journey Along the Line *by Colin Judge and E.R. Morten*

Published by
The Oakwood Press
P.O. Box 122, Headington, Oxford OX3 8LU

Contents

Introduction	5
Early History	6
Locomotives	17
Rolling Stock	27
The Route	35
The Line at Work	49
Towards the End	52
The Scene Today	55
Bibliography and Acknowledgements	64

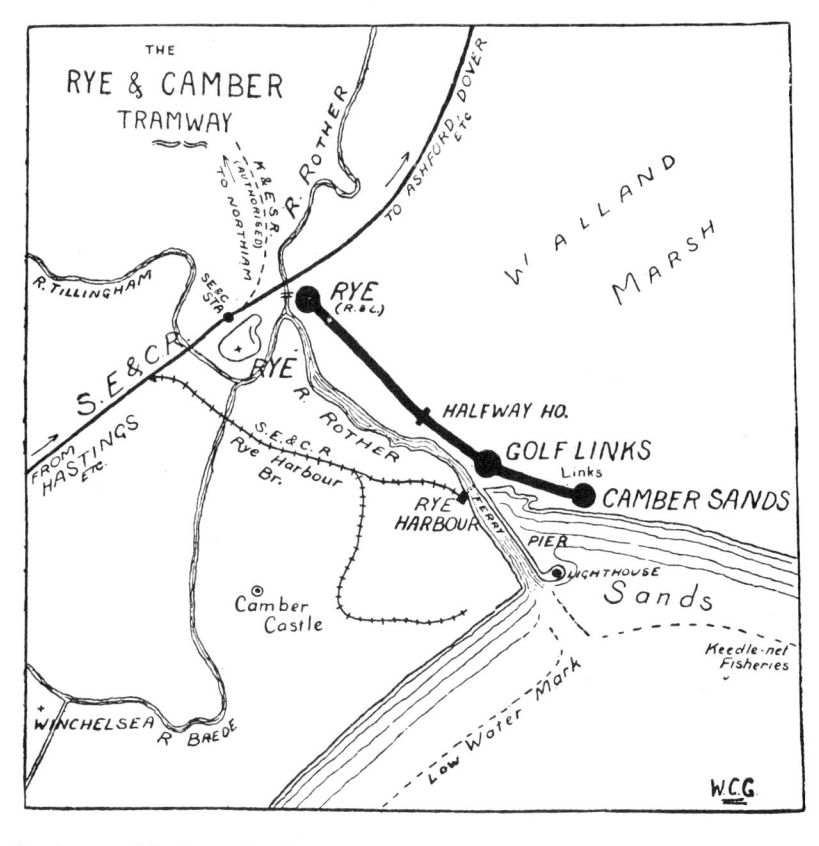

Sketch map of the Rye & Camber Tramway. *Courtesy Railway Magazine*

A superb photograph of the terminus at Rye, taken just before the opening of the line and deposited with the Board of Trade Inspecting Officer's report. The bridge in the background is Monkbretton bridge over the river Rother.
Public Record Office, Kew MT6/1966/4

Introduction

The Rye and Camber Tramway was a small and comparatively unknown 3 ft gauge 'steam' light railway (not a normal tramway), connecting the Cinque port of Rye in Sussex, with the splendidly wild and desolate area of sand dunes, under which the old town of Winchelsea was buried. The present town of the same name lies some three miles to the west and was built in the reign of Edward I.

An extract from the railway press of the 1890s, describes just one of the reasons why the tramway was constructed:

> The burgesses and fisherman of Rye have frequently to go to the harbour and also have to bring fish etc., from the boats to the town. Some enterprising gentlemen decided to construct a tramway to connect Rye town with the harbour.

The fisherman worked at the Keadle Net Fishery factory, where millions of mackerel were processed from the fleet of fishing boats that used Rye harbour. However many historians favour the idea that primarily the Tramway was constructed by the influence of wealthy locals who had just had built the golf course and clubhouse on Camber Sands and needed some form of transport to reach the same!

The line did not require any form of Parliamentary approval or powers, as it ran over private land; in fact it was never mentioned in the timetables of Bradshaw, and the local SECR ignored it in their timebook. Even the Rye Harbour waterway improvements of 1925-27 did not show the line on their detailed maps or mention it in their reports.

Run by very dedicated staff who took great pride in the line and stock, the Tramway boasted a very frequent and reliable service to the growing 'bungalow village' that was appearing on the Camber sands. Its early years of success allowed an extension to be built further into the area of Camber Sands and the original terminus of Camber, was then renamed Golf Links, this taking place in 1908. The Post Office made enquiries to the Board of Trade in 1911 as to the status of the Tramway as they wished to use it for carrying mail but the Board of Trade replied that 'no certificate of operation had been ever granted', so the idea was apparently dropped.

So this unique light railway, whose possible claim to fame was that it was one of the first, if not the first, public railway in the country to convert from steam traction to petrol, ran for 44 'accident free' years. The first passenger train entered service in 1895; the line extended to its full length in 1908 and it carried its last passengers in 1939. It was extensively used during World War II and from that experience it never recovered from the wear and neglect received and so faded into history, to become yet another railway of the past.

Today, it could have been a wonderful tourist attraction, with the slogan 'riding to the sands', as its catch line!

An old postcard view of one of the charming narrow streets of Rye.   *Author's Collection*

Early History

The town of Rye, situated in the south-east corner of beautiful Sussex, was on of the old Cinque ports. High on a hill of sandstone some 76 miles north-east from Chichester and 63 miles south-east from London, it looked down on the River Rother and across the surrounding marshes, sand and dunes towards the sea some two miles away.

In the reign of Edward III, the town was surrounded by a strong wall and several towers (erected by William of Ypres), one of which stands today and is called Ypres Tower. This tower was once a jail and was used to hold up to 12 persons.

In Edward's time, this port was very important and furnished nine warships for the invasion of France and when this battle was won, the returning Monarch landed at Rye port. However in the following reign the town was savagely burnt and plundered by the marauding French. By the reign of Elizabeth I, it was again a town and port of importance. Much later, in 1850, the River Rother had its watercourse cleared and deepened so that ships of 200 tons could navigate all the way up to the town's quay. The trade at that time was principally hops, corn, coal, bark, wool, timber, and chalk from the cliffs at Eastbourne, which was burnt locally to make lime. Fishing for herring, mackerel and flat fish were also important industries and the catches were mainly transported and sold in London. The port boasted 71 vessels (average 58 tons) being registered.

At the estuary to the River Rother, some two miles from Rye and on the west bank lies the village of Rye Harbour. As early as March 1854, the South Eastern Railway opened a standard gauge, single track branch line to the village from their Ashford to Hastings main line, which had been opened earlier on 13th

EARLY HISTORY

February, 1851. The Act for this branch line contained a clause stating that the SER should contribute £10,000 towards the development of the small harbour at Rye; the SER believed that the revenue from this branch about 1¾ miles long) would soon recompense this initial outlay. However throughout its history the line only carried limited freight and never had a passenger service. This being the case, it meant the fishermen still did not have any transport between the harbour and the town. However a stroke of luck came in 1894 when the Rye Golf Club and Course was founded and was constructed within the sand dunes opposite the harbour on the north-east bank of the River Rother. This prompted a group of local influential citizens to consider sponsoring a tramway, which would not only link the town to the golf course but also provide transport for the fishermen to Rye village and also to the Fishery factory nearby, albeit via a ferry across the Rother river.

After several public meetings in early 1895, Cuthbert Hayles was appointed to the chair and H.G. Henbrey, secretary. Early in March, the committee appointed Holman F. Stephens[*] of Light Railway construction fame, as the Company Engineer. Still in his twenties, Stephens wrote to the Board of Trade the following letter setting out the tramway's specification and construction details. One note of interest was that the motive power suggested was to be 'oil-motor', and if this had been implemented then the Rye and Camber would have had the first such passenger service in the world.[†] The Rye and Camber Tramway Company Ltd, was registered on 6th April, 1895 with a capital of £2,300, this being quickly subscribed and allocated to building and equipping the line.

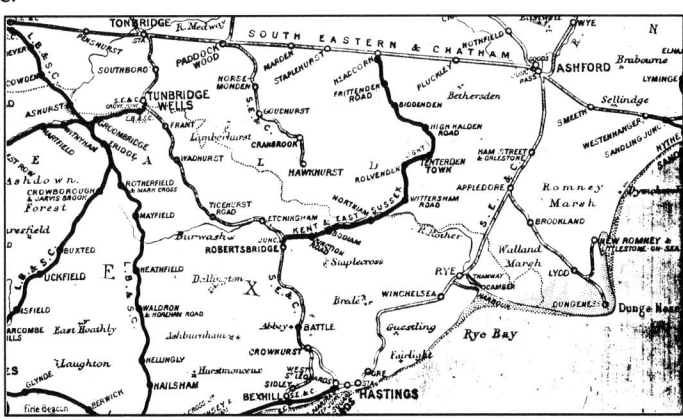

The RCH map of 1906 showing the railways surrounding the Tramway.

[*] Holman F. Stephens (1868-1931) first commission was the Cranbrook & Paddock Wood Railway before being appointed Engineer to the Rye and Camber Tramway. In 1895 he promoted a steam tramway from Sandwich to the golf course, which, however, was not constructed. In between these two appointments, he worked on the Medway Navigation Project. His full and fascinating history has been well documented (see Bibliography).
[†] *The Locomotive Magazine* of 15th September, 1922 stated that, 'Col Stephens arranged an old Priestman oil engine to drive a tramcar bogie', though an incorrect date is quoted. It was believed that Stephens was collaborating with Richard Hornsby & Son Ltd, Grantham, who built narrow gauge Hornsby-Ackroyd engines for the Royal Arsenal, in 1896. At that time all the oil engines required a spark or hot-tube for firing, so technically they were not diesels.

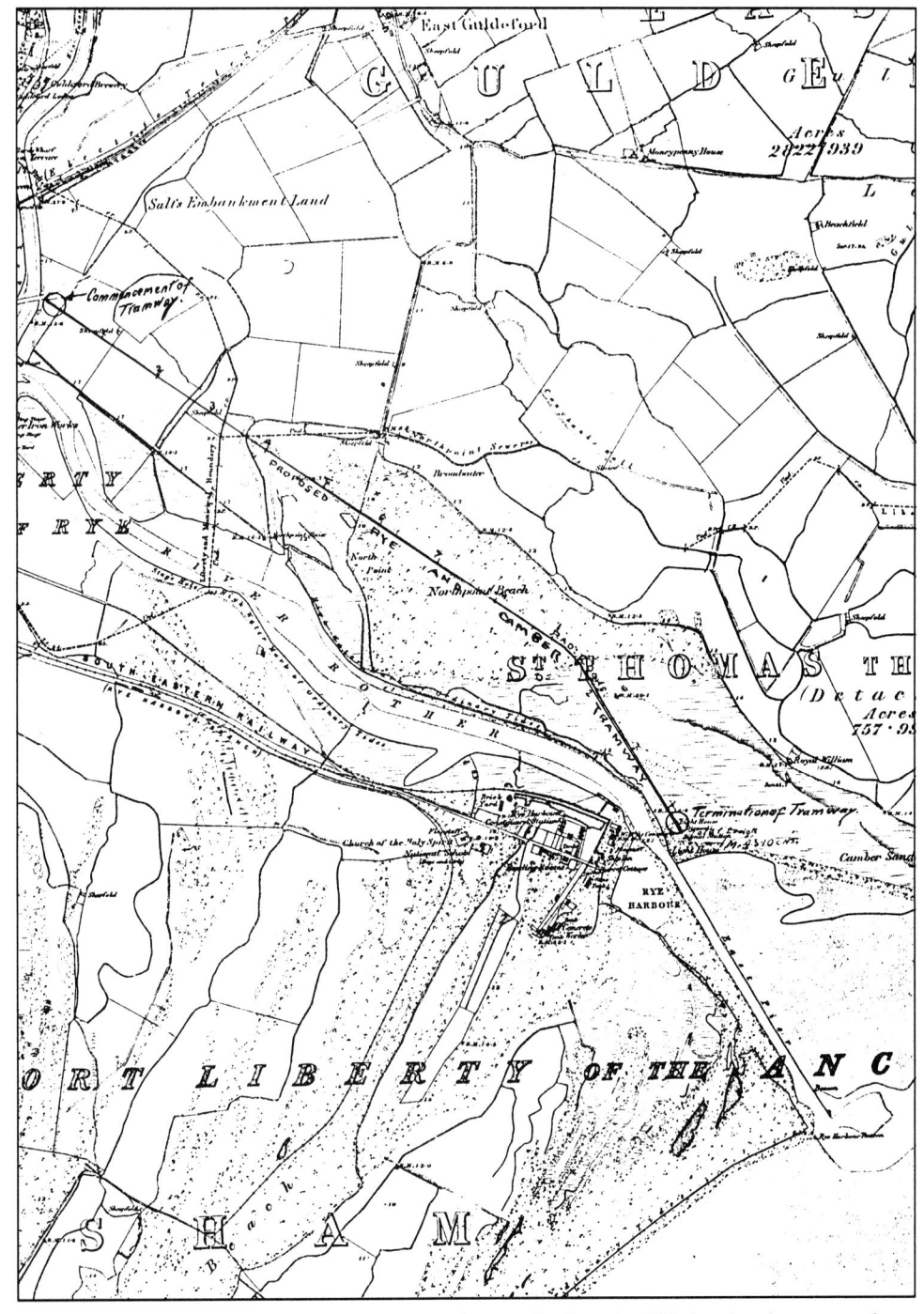

A reproduction of the original map submitted by H.F. Stephens in 1895 showing the proposed route of the Tramway; the actual route followed this proposal fairly closely.
Public Record Office, Kew MT6/1966/4

EARLY HISTORY

Rye and Camber Tramway
Cranbrook
Kent

Received 29 March 1895
No. 11869
Board of Trade

March 28th, 1895
To Asst Secy,
Railway Department
Board of Trade
London SW

Sir

In compliance with your suggestion expressed at our interview on Monday 25th inst.; I hereby forward to you particulars and plans of Rye & Camber Tramway (proposed).

The following figures are those upon which the Estimate was based: The P-Way will be laid with flat bottomed steel rails 24lbs per yard 3' 0" gauge with fish points spiked to sleepers: 2' 9" centre to centre: There will be a gradient of 1 in 100 for almost 10 chains in the centre and a curve of 20 chains radius at the harbour end for about 10 chains in length, the rest of the line will follow the surface of the land (which is marsh) and practically straight; there will be no cuttings other than 3' 0" deep and no bank more than 3' 6" high.

The power will be an oil motor on a passenger-bogie car with a load of not more than 1 ton per wheel or 2 ton per axle; with a wheel base of 20' 0".

The stations will be small corrugated iron shelters and the platforms 2' 0" above rail levels and 6' 0" wide and slightly longer than twice the length of the car.

There will be but one motor on the line and speed limited to 10 miles per hour or 4 per hour thro' points.

It is the wish of the Company not to fence the line, no public roads or footpaths are crossed.

The Company are anxious to use temporarily a small steam engine and car whilst the oil motor car is being constructed; or should the oil car not prove a success, then to work the line by steam.

There will be 3 small culverts of 15'-20' span, built with concrete walls and steel joists as rail bearers.

I should add that the funds are practically subscribed and the Company are anxious to proceed with the construction forthwith as it will enable work to be found for many men who are present unemployed.

I submit that the method of fastening rails altho' not in accordance with the Railway requirements of the Board, will be sufficient in the case of this tramway; when the weights are so small and the speed so slow.

I should be glad to furnish any further particulars you may desire or to call upon you and explain anything not being made clear and I trust you may see your way to approve of the above proposals.

I am
Sir,
Your obedient servant

The above is a transcript of a letter on file MT6/1966/4, Public Record Office, Kew from Col H.F. Stephens to the BOT.

Stephens, acting on behalf of the impatient Directors, hurriedly commissioned Mancktelow Brothers of Horsmonden as contractors to the scheme, who set about the task of laying 1¾ miles of track and erecting the two station buildings at Camber (later re-named Golf Links station in 1908) and Rye station sites. The costs and specification of the project is contained in a letter from J. Symonds-Vidlez to the Lord Advocates, dated 17th April, 1896.

April 17th, 1896

Dear Mr Murray
I have pleasure in forwarding you particulars of the Tramway at Rye.
1. Length of line, 1 Mile 31 chains 22 yards
2. Gauge - 3 ft. Weight of rails, 24lbs*
3. Cost of laying, including shed, 2 stations and fencing £1520
4. Cost of locomotive - £404 7s. 6d. nett
5. Cost of rolling stock - £288 nett†
The land is leased for 21 years at £8 per annum. This is all the trustees of Mr G. Carters had power to grant.
I shall be glad to give you any further particulars. Please address any further correspondence to Mountfield, Rye.
                                Yours,
                                J. Symonds Vidlez

As can be seen from the contents of the above letter, the authorised capital of £2,300 had been virtually consumed by the opening of the line so economy was the word of the day! The stations, as opened, had just simple run-round loops, with Rye terminus having a single road engine shed, a single platform with a canopy, a waiting room and booking office. These buildings were built of corrugated iron and wood, a construction generally favoured by Stephens and typical of the design used on the Kent and East Sussex Railway. The Rye town council had leased to the tramway company a small portion of the land near Monkbretton bridge for the position of the terminus (on the seaward side of the River Rother) at £2 per year, on a 21 year lease. At earlier consultation, the town council had requested a site nearer to the town, but this would have entailed constructing a bridge over the River Rother and so the cost prohibited this idea for such a small Tramway and the seaward site became the best option. This placed the terminus next to the main Dover road and to the river, being only 10 minutes walk from the SER's main line station.

So why a tramway and not a railway? The possible answer to that question is that the line was constructed on private land, with a lease of 21 years at £8 per annum rent (one presumes that the £2 Rye station site rent was a separate payment to this figure). The tramway was constructed quietly without Parliamentary approval and also was running before the Light Railway Act of 1896. If it had appeared after that date, it almost certainly would have been a Light Railway.

Several accounts of the line state that the single track system had no signals but only a telephone link between Rye and Golf Links stations. As the

* The official letter states 24lbs spiked rail (Vignoles rail, spiked to creosoted wooden sleepers), whereas all other printed references quote 26lbs.
† The one coach was £175, the rest of the cost was on two open wagons and a PW trolley.

EARLY HISTORY

telephone system was apparently not installed until 1904 in the area, it would appear that the tramway was operated on the 'one engine in steam' principle until the telephone link was established later on.

Construction was rapid and before the line was opened the BOT wrote on 5th July, 1895, to the Secretary of the Rye & Camber Tramway Co. Ltd as follows:

From Francis J. Hapwood, to the Secretary of Rye & Camber Trays. Co Ltd:

I am of the 29th ult. applying for inspection of the Rye and Camber Tramway which is proposed to open on the 13th inst. and I am to request that you will be good enough to state whether the Tramway is to be used for Goods Traffic only.

Being answered the next day:

6th July, 1895   From Faraday House, Rye   BOT 16397

Sir,
I am obliged by your favor [sic] of 5th July and beg to say the Tramway is being used for luggage and the Directors desire to open it for passenger traffic on Saturday next, 13th. I shall be glad to furnish you with any further information you may require.
H.G. Henbrey
Secretary

The opening ceremony took place on Saturday 13th July, 1895 and the following announcement appeared in the *Sussex Express*:

All arrangements have been made for the formal opening of the new tramway from Rye to Camber to-day (Saturday) at 1.45 pm, the Mayoress (Mrs Bellingham) having kindly consented to perform the interesting ceremony. The shareholders and their friends have also arranged to proceed to Camber over the line, and lunch together at the Royal William Hotel.* The train service will commence in the course of a few days, and we append the timetable, which, naturally is subject to alteration:

Leave Rye (*weekdays*) 8.20, 9.50, 11.20, 1.15, 2.00, 3.00, 4.00, 5.00, 6.00, 7.00 and 8.00.
Leaving Camber (*weekdays*) 8.40, 10.45, 12.30, 1.40, 2.30, 3.30, 4.30, 5.30, 6.30, 7.30 and 8.30.
Leave Rye (*Sundays*) 2.00, 2.30, 3.00, 4.00, 5.00, 6.00, 7.00, and 8,00.
Leave Camber (*Sundays*) 2.15, 2.45, 3.30, 4.30, 5.30, 6.30, 7.30 and 8.30.

The grand opening duly took place and the *Sussex Express* reported the event in its own descriptive way by stating that after the Mayoress received a bouquet from Miss Vidler, she declared the line officially open. To the loud sounds of fog-signal detonators and cheers from the large crowd, the first train, fully packed, 'chugged-off' to Camber terminus leaving yet a further contingent to travel on the second 'opening train'. When all were safely at Camber, they strolled across the Golf course to the Royal William Hotel for lunch and enjoyed a truly 'traditionally English Luncheon'. Many of the guests then set off to play a game of golf or stroll the sands and dunes before returning by a later train to the station at Rye.

Having only been delivered by the local haulier the day before, the

---
* Known locally as 'Old Billy'.

A heavily retouched commercial postcard showing the locomotive *Victoria* which has had the name *Camber* wrongly painted on the print, and the two coaches standing at the original Camber terminus during the early years. This view, taken prior to 1908, is one of the few to show the balcony open-end on the 'Jones' coach (second in the rake) and the handrail along the Bagnall coach. *H.C. Casserley Collection*

An early view of the locomotive *Camber* and coach at Rye terminus, believed to be taken just after the opening of the line. The locomotive livery shows up well in this view as does the central buffer and coupling. Note that all the windows have been removed from the second class section of the carriage, no doubt because of the hot weather. *Late R.C. Clarke Collection*

EARLY HISTORY

locomotive and carriage built by Bagnall's performed the opening service. The two goods wagons and permanent way trolley were held at Rye main line SER station for some days, before being delivered to the Rye Tramway at the terminus at Rye. The locomotive was aptly named *Camber* and is described later. Fares for the opening day were 4*d*. single and 6*d*. return for the first class seats and 2*d*. single and 4*d*. return for the second class accommodation. On offer was also a season ticket (mainly for the golfing fraternity). The local fisherman enjoyed a novel ticket which cost £1 10*s*. 0*d*. for an annual 'crew' ticket for their boat! It seems all went well for the first six months with over 18,000 tickets being sold, so allowing a dividend to be declared to the investors. The account and balance sheet is interesting and is reproduced on the next three pages.

Motive power and carriage seating capacity were stretched to their limit during these early days and so in 1896, a local company, the Rother Ironworks Co. Ltd, was commissioned to build a 25 seat, third class bogie coach based loosely on the Bagnall design. This locally was known as the 'Jones' coach, being named after E.P.S. Jones, who was the main carpenter involved in its construction. The lack of motive power was rectified in 1897 when yet another Bagnall-built locomotive arrived at Rye, this particular engine being slightly larger than *Camber* and named *Victoria*.

Taken in 1935, this view shows the terminus at Rye with the slogan 'TRAM TO CAMBER ON SEA'. Note the telegraph poles and wires which apparently carried all the lines to Camber Sands dwellings.
Roger Kidner

The RYE & CAMBER TRAMWAYS COMPANY,
LIMITED.

Report & Balance Sheet

NOTICE IS HEREBY GIVEN that an Ordinary General Meeting of the Members of the Rye and Camber Tramways Company, Limited, will be held at the Cinque Ports Hotel, Rye, on Friday, the 21st day of February, 1896, at 11 o'clock in the forenoon, to receive the Directors' Report and Accounts, to declare a dividend, to elect Directors and Auditors, and to transact the ordinary business of the Company.

By order of the Board,

H. G. HENBREY,
Secretary.

Faraday House,
Rye,
12th February, 1896.

ADAMS, PRINTER, RYE.

The front cover of the notice of the first General Meeting called for February 1896.

THE RYE AND CAMBER TRAMWAYS COMPANY,
LIMITED.

Directors.

R. T. BLOMFIELD.
R. P. BURRA.
C. HAYLES (Chairman).
F. A. INDERWICK.

C. A. SELMES.
T. G. SHARPE.
E. W. SKINNER.
J. S. VIDLER.

Report of the Directors

For the period ending 31st December, 1895, to be presented at the Annual Meeting of Shareholders to be held at the Cinque Ports Hotel, Rye, on Friday, the 21st February instant, at 11 o'clock in the forenoon.

The Directors herewith submit the accounts from the formation of the Company to the 31st December last, and are pleased to be able to report that the line has been an unqualified success since its opening on the 13th July last, the receipts from daily takings alone having amounted to £269 10s. 5d.

The net profit for the six months amounts to £83 3s. 2d., and out of this the Directors recommend that a dividend at the rate of 7½ per cent. per annum (from the dates of payment for the respective shares), which will absorb £43 3s. 4d., be declared and paid, and that the balance, after payment thereof and of any sum which the Shareholders may vote to the Directors for their services, be carried to a reserve fund.

The question of extending the line along the sandbanks has been fully considered by the Directors, and they are of opinion that it would be unwise to attempt it (at all events for the present).

The total cost of construction and equipment of the Tramway has not yet been arrived at, as a further sum will be due to the Contractor for the line and buildings on the Engineer's final certificate, and the Directors have also arranged for the building of another car, in consequence of the extent of the traffic, which has considerably exceeded their expectations.

Three of the Directors, Messrs. C. Hayles, F. A. Inderwick, and J. S. Vidler, and also the Auditors, Messrs. J. Adams and G. W. Strick, retire at this meeting, but are eligible and offer themselves for re-election.

(By order of the Board),

H. G. HENBREY,
Secretary.

The Rye and Camber Tramways Company, Limited.

N° 2313 BOARD OF TRADE

PROFIT AND LOSS ACCOUNT

For the 5½ months ended 31st December, 1895.

Dr.

	£ s. d.		£ s. d.
To Wages	73 6 6	By Fares	269 10 5
" Repairs and Stores	34 7 2	" Season Tickets	45 9 0
" Insurance	10 2 6		
" Coal	31 15 11		
" Rent, Rates, and Taxes	22 1 9		
" Printing, &c.	9 3 4		
" Sundries	10 16 3		
" Secretary, Salary	10 0 0		
" Balance, Gross Profit	114 6 1		
	£314 19 5		£314 19 5

	£ s. d.		£ s. d.
To Depreciation on Preliminary and Construction Expenses	19 8 10	By Balance, Gross Profit	114 6 1
" Interest on Debentures	11 14 1		
" Balance	83 3 2		
	£114 6 1		£114 6 1

BALANCE SHEET

From the 8th April, 1895, to the 31st December, 1895.

	£ s. d.		£ s. d.	£ s. d.
To Share Capital, 371 Shares at £3 10s.	1301 0 0	By Cost of Permanent Way and Rolling Stock to date	1878 5 7	
" Debenture Capital, 30 Debentures at £25	750 0 0	Less Amount paid by Rye Corporation for Fencing	50 0 0	1828 5 7
" Amounts owing on Construction Expense Account	96 0 8	By Preliminary and Construction Expenses, Engineer's Fees,		
" Amounts owing on General Expense Account	103 17 3	Law Costs, &c.	278 8 10	
" Balance	94 17 3	Less Depreciation	19 8 10	259 0 0
		" Account Owing		0 9 0
Less Interest on Debentures	11 14 1	" Balance at Bank		258 0 9
Net Balance	83 3 2			
	£2345 15 4			£2345 15 4

10th February, 1896.

Audited and found correct,

Locomotives

As previously stated, the first locomotive to be purchased by the Tramway was *Camber* at a cost of £404 7s. 6d. the official works' specification for this engine was :
Built by W.G. Bagnall Ltd of Stafford to works No. 1461, in the 'Concord' class.

Wheel arrangement	2-4-0T
Cylinders	5 in. x 9 in. outside cylinders
Leading Wheels	1 ft 0 in. dia.
Driving Wheels	1 ft 8 in. dia.
Wheelbase over mains	3 ft 0 in.
Total wheelbase	5 ft 6 in.
Water tank capacity	120 gallons
Working boiler pressure	140 lb. per sq. inch
Heating area:	
Tubes	55 sq. ft
Firebox	12 sq. ft
Grate area	2.5 sq. ft
Weight empty	5 ton 10 cwt.
Bunker capacity	13 cubic ft
Weight full	6 tons
Gauge of wheels	3 ft 0 in.

The locomotive was constructed with a telescopic boiler containing 26 fire tubes of 1¾ in. external diameter; the length of the boiler was 4 ft 3 in. and 1 ft 10 in. diameter inside the smallest ring and made of 5/16 in. plates. It was fed by two Gresham and Craven No. 3mm injectors with a Duplex Ramsbottom safety valve. The livery, as delivered, was an overall light green, with black bands and red lining. A special feature fitted to this locomotive was the side-sheets to cover the piston rods, slide blocks and little-ends as the sand blows continually across the open area of the dunes, even in a light breeze! It was alleged that *Camber* was capable of hauling 60 tons on the level at its normal speed of 10 mph, but was also capable of reaching around 20 mph, if 'flogged'! Other performance figures recorded are: 31 tons hauling capacity on an incline of 1 in 100, 17 tons on a 1 in 50 incline and nine tons on a 1 in 25 gradient. This engine was returned to Bagnall's in 1926 for repairs, then again in 1931 for a complete rebuild as works No. 2313 and finally scrapped at Rye in 1947. It was certainly inside the shed at Rye terminus in April 1946, as several photographs record it there.

The second locomotive named *Victoria* was also built by W.G. Bagnall Ltd, Stafford to works No. 1511 and delivered to the Rye and Camber Tramway Co. Ltd, in June 1897 and on paper appeared to be more powerful than its predecessor.

Wheel arrangement	2-4-0T
Cylinders	6 in. x 10 in. outside cylinders
Leading Wheels	2 ft 0½ in. dia.
Driving Wheels	1 ft 2 in. dia.
Wheelbase over mains	3 ft 0 in.

A fine detailed view of the 2-4-0T locomotive *Camber* standing alongside the two coaches at Rye terminus.

The late F. Moore Collection

A posed photograph at the original Camber terminus (to become Golf Links station later). Here 2-4-0T *Camber* stands with driver Albert Rhodes (nicknamed 'Jokey'). Guard/conductor Percy Sheppard standing down on the track remained with the tramway until its closure in 1939, when he joined the Southern Railway. *H.C. Casserley Collection*

Another look at the locomotive *Camber* showing front detail, with the 0-4-0 petrol locomotive in the background, photographed at Rye terminus. *Real Photographs*

The 2-4-0T locomotive *Victoria* standing at Rye terminus. This view shows clearly the smaller and compact sand-covers over the slide rods and also the locally made plate to cover up the bottom half of the door.

H.C. Casserley Collection

Dejected guard Percy Sheppard stands in front of the locomotive *Victoria* at Golf Links station on 10th April, 1909. Perhaps trade was not so good that day!
Ken Nunn Collection/LCGB No. H2084

A wet day at Rye terminus with 2-4-0T *Victoria* standing unoccupied alongside the coal dump. This view taken on 18th July, 1914, shows how the cab door has been completely covered in to keep out the biting winds and rain that were a feature of this area both in summer and winter.
Ken Nunn Collection/LCGB No. 1816

This view taken at Rye terminus on 10th April, 1909 of both the two steam locomotives, *Camber* and *Victoria*, allows the reader to compare the relative sizes of the engines. Note the carriage shed had not been constructed at this time.
H.C. Casserley Collection

LOCOMOTIVES

Wheelbase	3 ft 3 in.
Total wheelbase	6 ft 5½ in.
Water tank capacity	150 gallons
Working Pressure	140 lb. psi
Heating area:	
Tubes	103 sq. ft
Firebox	15 sq. ft
Grate area	3 sq. ft
Weight empty	6 ton
Weight Full	6 ton 12 cwt.
Bunker capacity	16 cubic ft

This locomotive was also fitted with a Bagnall telescopic boiler which contained 45 tubes of 1¾ in. external diameter, the length being 4 ft 9 in. and 2 ft 1⅜ in. dia. inside the smallest ring and made of ⁵⁄₁₆ in. plate. Again this locomotive was fed by two Gresham and Craven No. 3mm injectors with a Duplex Ramsbottom safety valve. The livery as delivered, was overall blue (similar to the LNER standard blue) and chrome-yellow lining.

Protective side plates were fitted over the motion to keep out the abrasive sand particles, but these were of a better design and standard than those on *Camber*. She was sold in 1937 to an unknown purchaser.

The Tramway introduced a 4-wheel petrol locomotive in 1925, being built by the Kent Construction and Engineering Co. Ltd, Ashford, Kent to works No. 1364 and fitted with a Dorman petrol engine and when delivered the locomotive was painted dark green. This locomotive had a small half-width cab when originally built, for the driver to sit sideways with his feet exposed, but later it was rebuilt with a full cab which, however, was changed several times, as can be seen in the accompanying photographs. The driver was equipped with a system of wires, which, when pulled from inside the cab, released the pin from the centre of the coupling, so releasing the coaches from the locomotive and allowing it to run-round its train without the driver having to get out of the cab! It was finally scrapped in October 1946.

It is interesting to note that the Rev. J.E. Anderson, whose father built a bungalow in 1911, 50 yards from the tramway on the edge of the golf links, stated in 1974 that when he was a boy there a third engine was used occasionally, which he thought was called *Coronation*. It was painted grey as against the bright green of *Camber* and bluish green of *Victoria*. However no other reference can be found relating to this locomotive.

The 4wP locomotive (seen here on 29th August, 1931) supplied by the Kent Construction and Engineering Company Limited to the Rye and Camber Tramway. The locomotive had a small half cab when built, but the tramway converted this to a full cab with the one square look out window and small side window. Note the covers over the wheel bearings.
Ken Nunn Collection/ LCGB No. 5897

This slightly later view shows that the cab side window has been changed to a fixed window and allows the reader to see the details of the engine, including the starting handle.
Real Photographs

The locomotive was then given a general overhaul during 1936 and received round spectacle windows both front and back, plus a small square window in the side. Note the wheel bearing covers have been removed.
Real Photographs

The last view of the 4wP locomotive taken in 1937 shows the cab changes and the addition of a sand box for better traction. The vehicle had also recently received a new coat of paint.
Photomatic Ltd

Locomotive *Victoria* at Rye terminus with both coaches. Note the novel advertising painted on the roof of the buildings. The Bagnall coach still has the balconies at either end, and the 'Jones' coach just one in this 1910 view. Note the lean-to shed has yet to be added to the end of the building, named 'station, nor has the two-road carriage shed been built.

Real Photographs

Rolling Stock

Coaches

The first passenger coach was supplied new from W.G. Bagnall Ltd with the first locomotive and is reported to have cost £175. It had two open-end platforms with a central entrance either end into the carriage, but a door was fitted to the first class end. This compartment had 12 cushioned seats situated along the side of the coach and across the central division which divided the coach into two. This partition had an unusual feature in that a clock was fixed to the partition on the first class side. Curtains were also provided. The second class area seated 20 people utilising longitudinal strip-wood seating. All the windows were sash-type and could be completely removed in hot weather. Lighting was by two oil lamps and braking by a handbrake. It was rebuilt around 1925, when the winter services ceased and during this rebuild all the handrails, oil lamps and brake gear were removed. The end platforms were totally enclosed and some windows altered, with a doorway being cut through the middle partition to make just one class, third class! The first class door was panelled in and a sliding door placed on the side entrance to the former second class end.

The outside was constructed using straight down matchboard sides enclosed by 1½ in. x 1½ in. angle iron ¾ in. thick. These angles were fitted on both sides of the former 1st class end and on one side of the 2nd class end and they projected beyond the body by ¾ in., making the actual overall length 25 ft 9 in. and the width 5 ft 9 in.

Dimensions

Weight	3 tons (approx.)
Length	25 ft 7½ in.
Height	9 ft 0½ in.
Width	5 ft 7½ in.
Bogies...Wheelbase	12 ft 6 in.
Wheel Centres	3 ft 6½ in.
Wheel Dia.	1 ft 2½ in., seven curved spokes
Springing	Coil Springs
Couplings	Centre buffer, pin & link plus safety chain
Buffers	Central, no outside buffers fitted
Livery	Maroon body and light grey roof

The coach was sold locally and used as a chicken shed as East Guldeford, during the 1960s, the Brockham Museum Association in Surrey added this dilapidated vehicle to their collection. Since then the vehicle has been removed to the Chalk Pits Museum, Sussex awaiting complete restoration.

The second coach used on the line was locally built in 1896, at the Rother Ironworks which was situated just down the road from the terminus at Rye. The head carpenter, E.P.S. Jones of the iron works, used the Bagnall coach as a master and virtually copied it, however making the body into 3rd class to accommodate 25 passengers. Access was via a platform at one end only and the carriage had three large side windows capped by ventilators. This coach also was rebuilt and the balcony removed and the doors placed on the platform side only (as with the original Bagnall coach). The construction of the bogies was

The original coach built by Bagnall's photographed prior to its rebuilding in 1925, showing clearly the curtains, the balconies, oil lamps, the partition inside and bogie detail. One report stated that an outside running board was provided for the conductor to take fares whilst the train was running, but no evidence or photographs show this. However a handrail is evident, but it has been removed in this view.

Author's Collection

An unusual view taken from the platform side at Rye terminus showing Rye Town in the background. Locomotive *Camber* 2-4-0T, stands with the two coaches that are about to be pushed back into the platform and the unusual permanent way trolley appears in the foreground. The coaches at this time were fitted with sliding doors and the balconies enclosed, which can be seen in the photograph. *Author's Collection*

Both the coaches again appear on a train with the diminutive 4wP locomotive in charge. The second coach (built locally and known as the 'Jones' coach) is at the back of the train. The fencing seems to have been become dilapidated, and the paintwork is fading from the station roof. *Steam Chest Publications*

A further postcard view taken again from the platform side at Rye terminus, showing the two coaches and the tiny 4wP locomotive. Note the completely open side to the cab on the engine.
Lens of Sutton

The two special open wagons converted into coaches are seen here at Camber Sands mustered with the two standard coaches giving maximum seating capacity during the summer months. The style of seats and opening doors in the sides to these vehicles (on the platform side only) can be clearly seen.
Steam Chest Publications

A rare view of the original wagons as supplied to the tramway, with their small and flimsy wheels.
Author's Collection

The two open wagons standing on the single siding at Rye terminus photographed on 10th April, 1909. Note the pieces of cloth hanging down over the axleboxes to avoid sand entering the grease in the bearings. This siding was replaced by two sidings and the covered carriage shed.
Ken Nunn Collection/LCGB No. H2088

A detailed view of the pump handle permanent way trolley. *Author's Collection*

again a copy from the Bagnall original coach. This coach, as stated previously, was known affectionately as the 'Jones' coach.

Two further 'coaches' were added to the fleet after World War I, when two open wagons (that had been used for the transportation of ammunition), were converted locally into open carriages by fitting bench seats across them. They were fairly high sided with small doors fitted on the station side of the wagon and seated 20 passengers in five transverse seats, across the wagon.

Wagons

The original two wagons that were purchased at the commencement of the railway were very flimsy indeed, as can be seen from the accompanying photograph. These were replaced by two much more substantial, 4-plank open wagons in early 1900 and used mainly to convey sand to Rye from the Camber beach, for use by local builders. They were also used for carrying fish and parcels. The parcel service had an overall charge of 4d. per consignment, which included the travel on the Tramway, a ferry crossing, and delivery to its destination in the village of Rye Harbour. The wagon could be hired for just 1s. 0d. They also were used later to convey fresh water to the inhabitants on Camber Sands itself.

Permanent Way Trolley

This was a four-wheeled vehicle with a 'rowing-boat' action handle (*see photograph*) and was probably made especially for the Tramway, due to the gauge. Apparently 'Pa Rhodes' would stop this trolley at the bungalow of the Rev. J.E. Anderson and allow him and his brother to ride the trolley and work the crank handles.

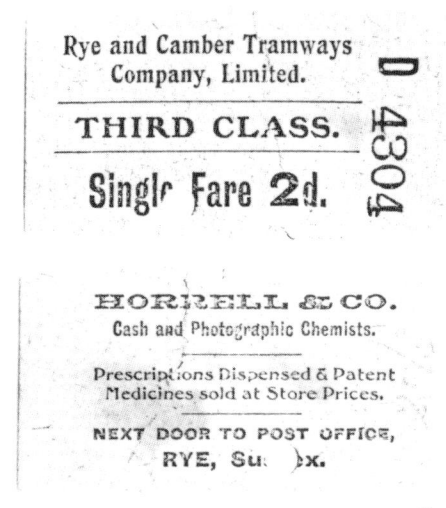

Colour of ticket, blue. *Courtesy: Premier Tickets*

A view of Rye terminus taken in the 1930s which should be compared with that on *page four*. An extra building and lean-to shed has been added to the station building and an open shed added between the engine shed and station platform. The water tank on top of the engine shed has been removed.
Robert Humm

A scene on 11th April, 1931, of the whole station area at Rye terminus, seen from the road. The infill shed (used for storage of the carriages) beside the engine shed (which had been extended by half its original length) can clearly be seen.
H.C. Casserley

The Route

The terminus buildings situated by Monkbretton Bridge, Rye, were constructed of corrugated iron on a wooden framework and incorporated ornate and decorative barge boards, typical of the 'Stephens' design of the period. They contained initially a waiting room and ticket office; the latter not being used soon after the opening of the line, as the tickets were sold by the conductor/guard on the train. At the time of the opening, a single-road engine shed and station building were all that existed but later a double-road carriage shed, plus a small wagon shed were constructed all to a similar style. Even later a further open-ended shed was built at the end of the running line. The platform was surprisingly constructed of concrete, faced with brick on the top edge. The early photograph at the front of the book, shows the station fencing and the seats, plus detail of the point switching levers.

From Rye terminus the 3 ft gauge line travelled south-eastwards in a straight line for about 700 yards on a level gradient then turned 10° eastwards for a further 200 yards before crossing a bridge over Broadwater stream (the first quarter of a mile of the track had to be fenced under the original leasing agreement and boasted a sturdy iron posted fence, on both sides). The line then continued a further 500 yards before coming back to its original heading and then ran a further 800 yards to the first house to be encountered on the route. This building was called Gorse Cottage and was situated on the right-hand side of the track, however about 100 yards further on (this time on the left-hand side) another building was passed, named Golf View (*now demolished*).

All this section of the track ran on an open area of land/shingle and was unfenced. This point along the route was not listed in the timetables but trains would stop here if requested, although no platform was provided, being called 'Halfway House'. Another cottage appeared on the left-hand side, which was at one time home to the Rye Harbour Master, Charles Tunbridge. The line curved further round towards the south and after about 400 yards ran into the original terminus of Camber station. This station was similar in design to Rye, with its concrete and brick platform, station building and run-round loop; however this loop was removed in the 1930s, as it was hardly used after the extension of the line to Camber Sands in 1908. The station was then renamed Golf Links station. During World War II the loop was reinstated and a further branch line to the jetty on the River Rother nearby added for use by the Admiralty. The steps today are called Jetty steps and here was sited a ferry across the river to Rye Harbour village. After the extension of the line in 1908, the line ran a further 850 yds, in part on a small embankment curving round in an easterly direction to the new terminus at Camber Sands. This station was a 'let-down', being crudely constructed of old standard gauge sleepers and a wooden shed for the waiting room and passenger shelter. A run-round loop was provided and the line did in fact continue past the station for about 90 yards running right up to the dunes. This terminus was sometimes referred to as being 'far from the madding crowds'. Being well over half a mile from Camber, with no road or footpath to it, this statement was somewhat accurate! Over the years of the Tramway's existence, a tea room was provided by a local business man in this wild, but idyllic, area, where the golden sands and dunes stretched for miles.

Locomotive *Victoria* runs into Rye terminus on the 1.45 pm from Golf Links on 18th July, 1914. Note the virtually straight-sided smokebox compared to the curved and waisted shape of *Camber*. This view looks along the straight and fenced section of the route towards Golf Links station.
Ken Nunn Collection/LCGB No. 614

On the same day, but further along the track, the 3.35 pm from Golf Links service passes over the bridge which carried the Tramway over the Broadwater stream. In both views Percy Sheppard (guard) keeps a good watch out from the balcony of the Bagnall coach.
Ken Nunn Collection/LCGB No. 616

Rye Terminus

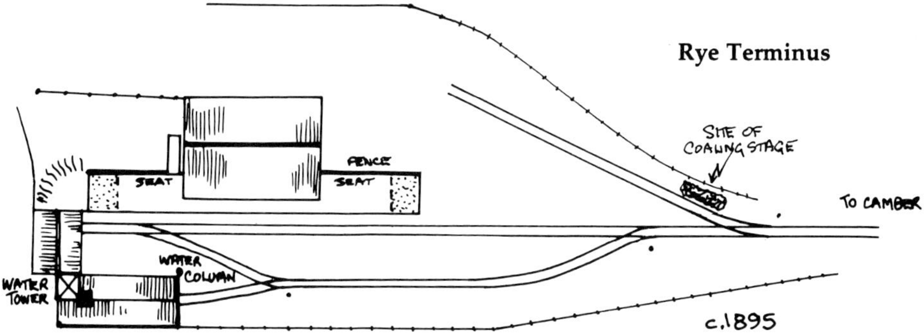

Rye Terminus

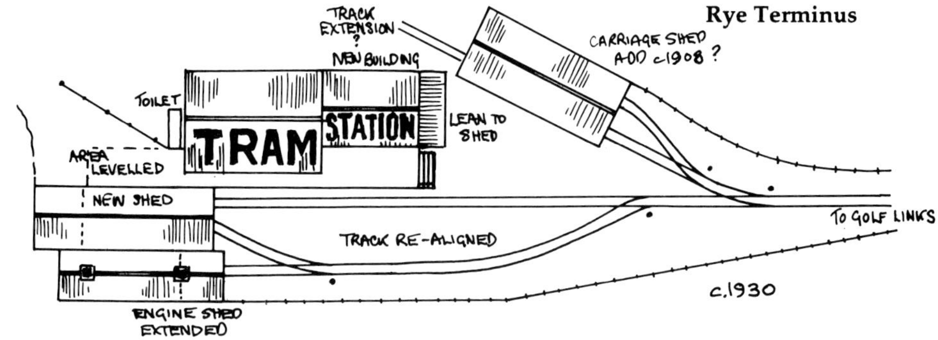

Golf Links

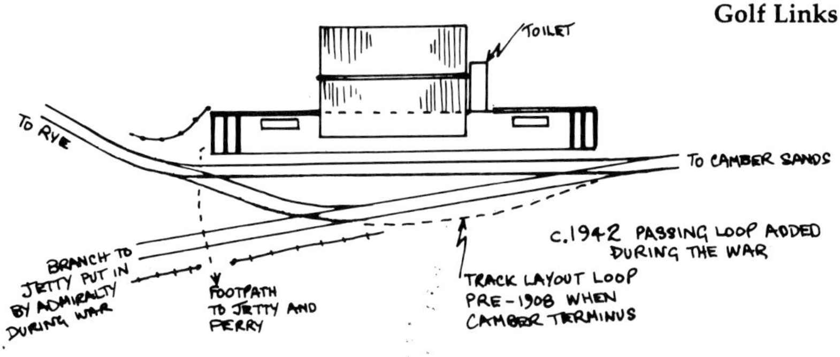

Camber Sands

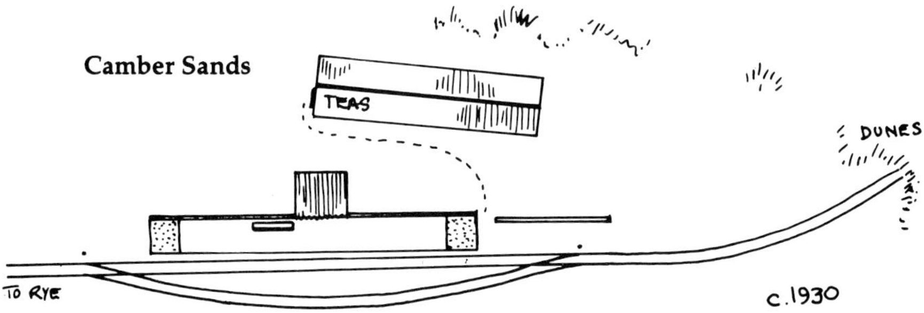

All diagrammatic and not to scale; drawn from photographic evidence.

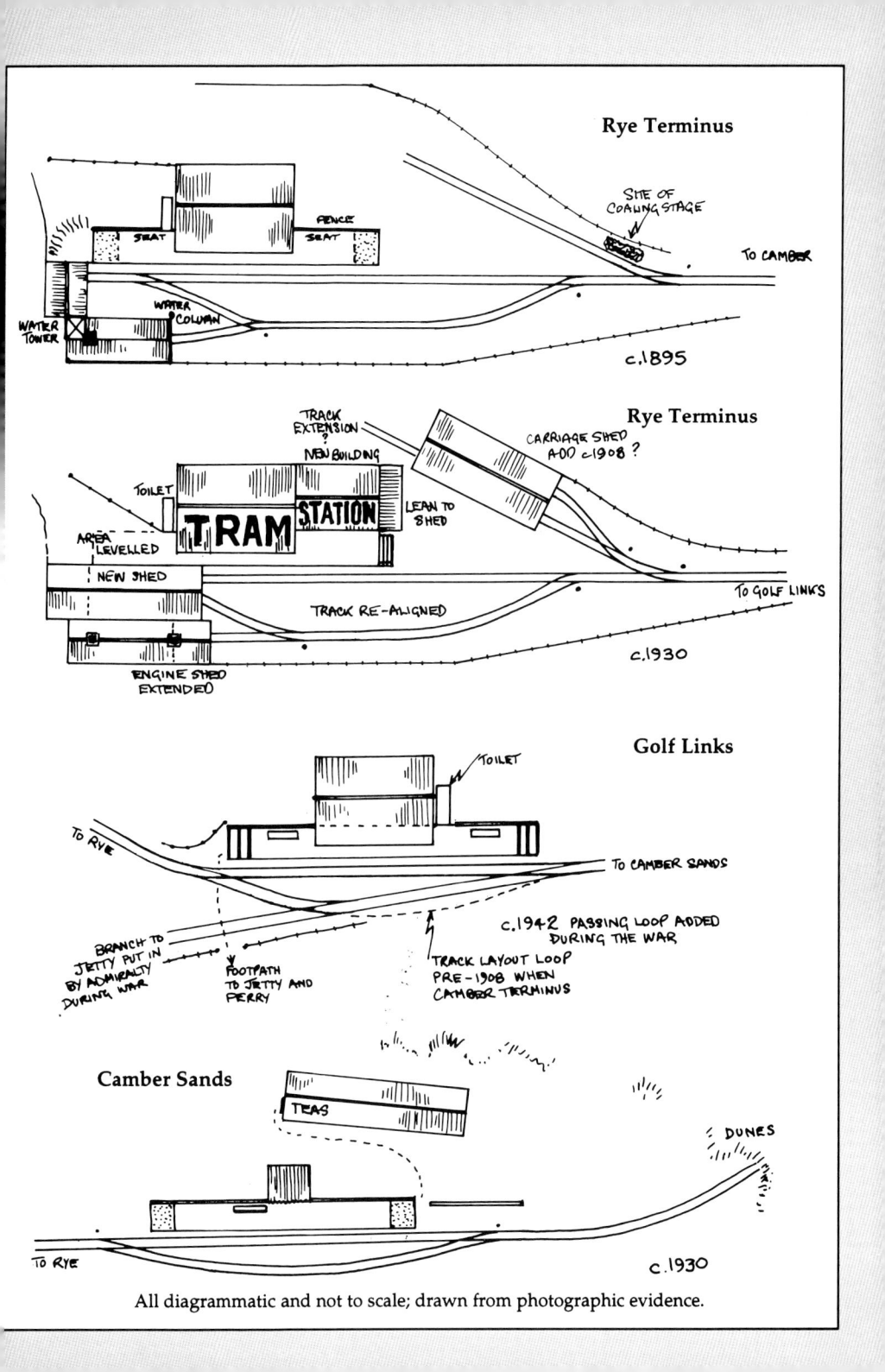

The map on these pages shows the complete route of the Rye and Camber Tramway. The inset *(bottom left)* shows Rye town and the position of the SE&CR station. The main line company's harbour branch can also be clearly seen.

Reproduced from the 1906, 25 in. Ordnance Survey map, courtesy Ordnance Survey

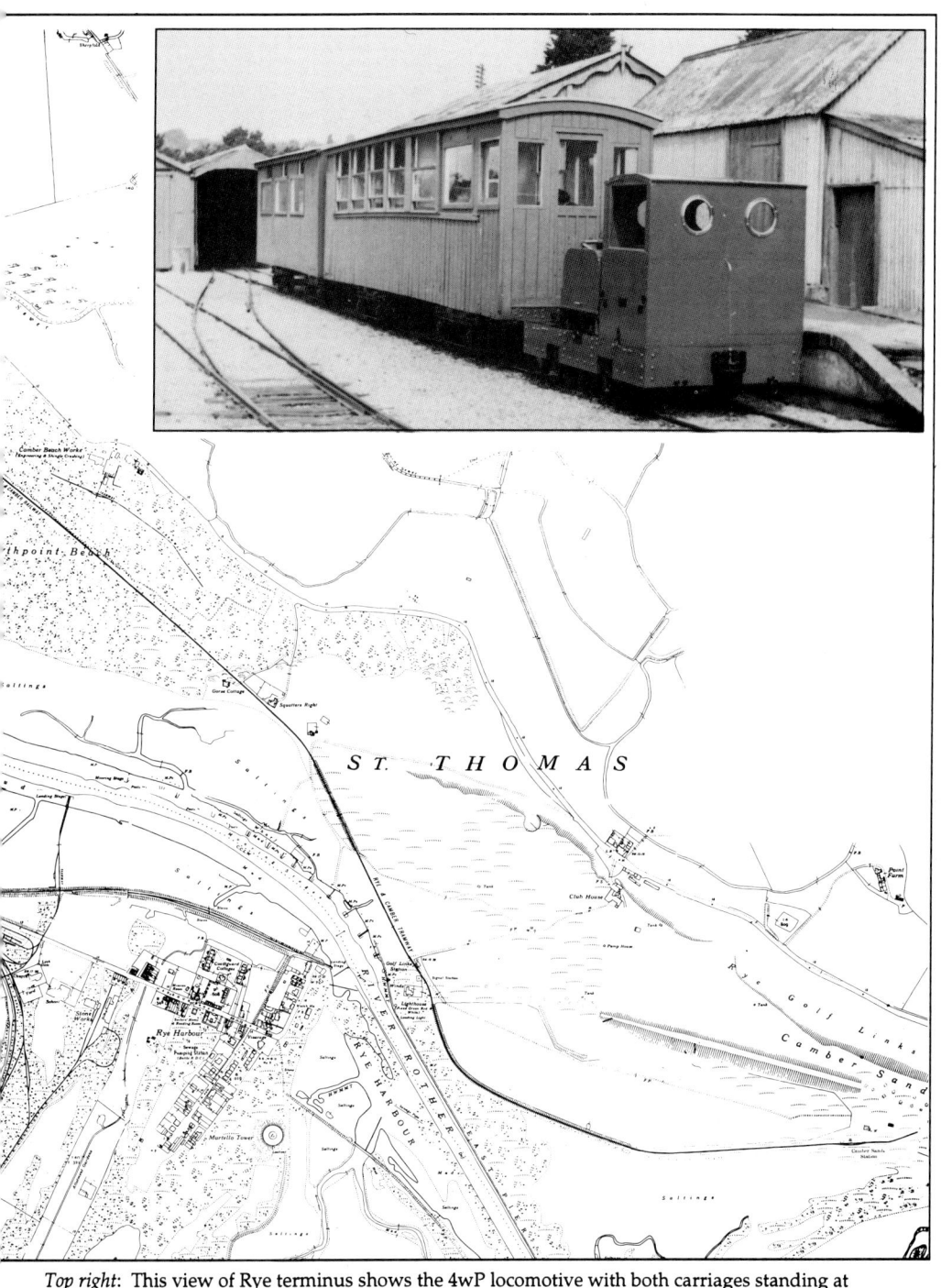

Top right: This view of Rye terminus shows the 4wP locomotive with both carriages standing at the platform. Details of the coaches are clearly seen in this view. *Robert Humm*

In the 1930s, there were two shingle-digging companies with tramways on the North Beach area between Rye and Halfway House. One ran under the Rye and Camber Tramway by a makeshift bridge and here in 1934, one of the locomotives hauls a good load on one of the shingle tramways. This area is now used by film and TV companies for shooting desert scenes!
Roger Kidner

The original Camber Sands terminus *c.* 1900. Locomotive *Camber* has just arrived from Rye with both coaches. The 'Jones' coach is nearest to the engine.
R. Walmsley/Adrian Vaughan Collection

Two more views of the original terminus of the tramway at Camber Sands, these being taken in 1909, just after the extension was opened, hence the station bearing the new name Golf Links. The passing loop is still *in situ* and in the upper view the lighthouse consisted of a fixed green, red and white light. Note the break in the fence and the path leading off right to the ferry across the River Rother. Detail of the platform and fencing are similar to the terminus at Rye.
Top photograph: Real Photographs and lower: Ken Nunn Collection/LCGB No. H2089

Golf Links station on 12th July, 1931 looking back towards Rye with Golf View house clearly visible. Note the Tramway runs on a small embankment at

This view of Golf Links station taken on the same day looks towards Camber Sands. The passing loop has been removed, so has the toilet alongside the station building and the wooden buildings in the distance have also been pulled down. *H.C. Casserley*

From the other side of the River Rother, at the end of the standard gauge Rye Harbour branch, this 1958 view shows the abandoned and derelict Golf Links station in the middle and the Harbour Master's house on the right, *Roger Kidner*

Rye and Camber Tram, Rye. 15.

With the 2-4-0T *Victoria* at its head, this full-to-capacity train utilises the two main coaches plus the two converted open wagons and is here seen just leaving Camber Sands.

Roger Kidner Collection

A view on 12th July, 1931 of another well-loaded train coming around the curve and into Golf Links station, with Camber Sands in the distance, on the extreme left.   *H.C. Casserley*

This was the 'new' terminus at Camber Sands and this view shows just how rough and ready it was. On a wet day the passengers certainly would have to compete to keep dry! The wooden building in the background became a tea room.

Heyday Publishing Company

Locomotive *Victoria* with both coaches at Camber Sands, soon after the extension was completed.

The late F. Moore Collection

The 4wP locomotive stands at the desolate Camber Sands with two coaches, waiting to take out a fairly full 4.25 pm service to Rye, on 29th August, 1931. *Ken Nunn/LCGB No. 5899*

Locomotive *Victoria* stands simmering at Camber sands with a few passengers looking out of the Bagnall coach, waiting for the 'off'. Note the large sack of coal on the platform and the Tea Room in the distance. *Real Photographs*

Driver George Wratten talks with a group of small interested children, whilst the dog couldn't care less! The petrol engine awaits on 12th July, 1931 to transport its passengers back to Rye. Note again the detailed construction of the station.
H.C. Casserley

The Line at Work

After the first six months, the line settled down to a modest success story and during this period *Camber* ran some 7,000 miles at a cost of approximately £200 (2.85*d*. per mile).

In 1901, the East Sussex Light Railway Order was authorised for the construction of a standard gauge line from the Rother Valley Light Railway at Northiam to Rye station on the SECR. Section 38 of this order gave the light railway the powers to maintain, repair and even work the Rye and Camber Tramway; a strange situation as there was no physical connection of the two railways envisaged, however the line never materialised and so the Rye and Camber continued its life in its own quiet way.

On the company's 13th birthday, 13th July, 1908, it celebrated the occasion with the opening of the half-mile extension to the new terminus at Camber Sands. The *Sussex Express* for 18th July, 1908, carried the following report of the occasion:

The long talked of extension of the Rye and Camber Tramway's line is now an accomplished fact, and the formal opening took place on Monday afternoon when about 50 of the Directors, shareholders and Town Councillors travelled down by special train. Amongst those present were; Mr Cuthbert Hayles (Chairman of the Company), Aldermen J.N. Masters, F. Jarrett, Rev. W.M. Manning, Messrs A.A. Clarke JP, G. Ellis JP, Walter Dawes, E.P. Dawes, R.H. Hunnisett (Managing Director) etc. The actual ceremony of opening the extension was performed by the train itself breaking a silken cord stretched across the line just beyond the point to where the line originally terminated. On arrival at Camber Sands station, the company halted for a short time, and on returning to the Retreat, tea was served. The Chairman, in the course of a short speech, then referred to the length of time which the tramway had been running, and he considered that the public would materially benefit as a result of the extension, as they could now be taken right on to the seashore. The cost of the undertaking was £650, and the greater amount of this had been readily taken up in debentures. Mr Walter Dawes proposed the health of the Chairman and Directors and said he thought the extension had been very good speculation on the part of the Company. Major Vidler replied and referred to the enhanced value of the land which had been reclaimed as a result of the extension. Ald. Masters proposed a vote of thanks to the debenture holders, and Mr A.A. Clark JP, replied on their behalf. Major Selmes proposed 'The Ladies' and Liet E.P. Davies responded. A vote of thanks to the Chairman brought the gathering to a close.

Many local people were under the impression that the new terminus was situated in the position it was, only because of the rails running out, as it sat in the middle of nowhere!

The fares were altered accordingly, the first class fare being 6*d*. single to Golf Links and Camber and 9*d*. return; second class 3*d*. to Golf Links and 6*d*. return and 4*d*. to Camber Sands and 7*d*. return. A third class fare was available at 2*d*. to Golf Links and 3*d*. to Camber Sands and 5*d*. return from both destinations. A special cheap return ticket of 2*d*. to Golf Links was available for golf caddies, children and dogs. An innovation was a book of tickets giving 2 shillings discount on 40 x 6*d*. tickets, as was a large reduction for two season tickets from one household: first class (one person) 30 shillings and second class (two persons from one household) 42 shillings. Lastly cheap season tickets were issued to operating crews.

The frequency of service on the line before the extension was 10 trains each way (June 1908), with two extra trains on Saturdays. The Sunday service had nine trains each way. In 1912, the service had increased to a high level of 13 trains daily each way, but only seven proceeding through to the terminus at Camber Sands. The trip took eight minutes to Golf Links and then six minutes to Camber Sands terminus. Apparently the influence of the Golf Club ensured that a late train (8.15 pm) ran on Saturdays for the benefit of patrons of the 'nineteenth hole'. On Sundays the service consisted of nine trains each way to Golf Links with five proceeding right through to the terminus.

The winter timetable for 1912 showed seven trains each way to the Golf Links station, with nine on Saturdays and four on Sunday, however none continued through to the terminus at Camber Sands.

By 1925, only eight trips ran on weekdays and seven on Sundays with the proviso added to the published timetable that 'Special trains would be laid on for more than 12 passengers'.

During the winter months, the Tramway suffered crippling cash flow problems and as early as October 1903 the local *Sussex Express* reported:

> Some weeks ago we announced the decision of the Directors of the Rye and Camber Tramway not to run their steam cars throughout the winter months unless they received a subsidy of £50 to enable them to recoup themselves for the loss which would thus be involved. Since then the matter has been put before various clubs in the town, with the result that a meeting of the Directors on Saturday, the Secretary was able to state that the Golf, Mermaid and Dormy Clubs had guaranteed to pay two-thirds of the amount required, whilst the Mayor (Dr Skinner) had guaranteed the other third. Accordingly the trams will continue to run as hitherto, and the Mayor's generous action will earn the gratitude of the townspeople, who will thus be enabled to easily reach the sea throughout the winter, whilst it will be an equal boon to the residents at the Harbour, The Mayor's action is not, however, without a precedent, for in 1900 the then Mayor (Ald. F. Jarrett), benefited the town in a similar manner.

This shows that from the early years of the Tramway, the winter services were sponsored by the local establishments and the main contributor appeared to be the Golf Club, who obviously had the most to gain. Between 1917 and 1924, a figure of £25 annually was agreed and in 1925 this sum was increased to £38, but in the following year this was discontinued and winter operations ceased in 1926.

To help with the ailing cash flow in 1925, the company introduced an experimental petrol driven 0-4-0 locomotive which was constructed at the Kent Construction and Engineering Co. Ltd. Although this vehicle was often referred to as an overgrown lawn mower, it proved very successful and economical, so much so that the steam locomotive *Victoria* was sold in 1937 and *Camber* was exiled to the locomotive shed after its works service in 1931 and was seldom seen running. It was finally sold in 1947 for scrap.

From contemporary reports the Tramway's locomotives and rolling stock were kept in very good condition and the staff were smartly attired. During the summer months in the 1930s, the driver-conductor would sport grey flannels and a white yachting cap.

CAMBER SANDS.
Scene at official opening of the Tramways Extension.

The large crowds at the official opening of the Tramway's extension on 13th July, 1908 at the new station at Camber Sands. *Courtesy Railway Magazine*

18th July, 1914 was a fine summer's day and a young girl's school party waits for the locomotive *Victoria* to run round its train before being allowed to join the coaches by guard Percy Sheppard.
Ken Nunn Collection/LCGB No. 1812

Towards the End

During the early 1930s, a motor bus service was introduced between Rye Town and Camber and as with many other branch lines and rural lines throughout the country, the Tramway began to feel the pinch even more. As one elderly lady said: 'The seats were softer, there was less noise and there was the distinct advantage of catching the bus from the centre of Camber and being deposited "up the hill" in the centre of Rye, and you didn't get wet!' So the new form of transport had arrived and the Tramway's revenue now came mainly from the day trippers to Camber Sands, rather than the golfers, who now seemed to be acquiring their own motor vehicles. It is interesting to note that the Southern Railway carried out a feasibility exercise with the idea of joining the tramway to their main line, so encouraging more 'through' traffic to the sands! However the difference in the gauges and the heavy expense of constructing a bridge over the River Rother ensured that the scheme was never really seriously considered.

In the early 1930s, a shingle works was situated at Camber Sands under the ownership of W.E. Colebrooke & Co. Ltd and they operated a 2 ft gauge railway with a PAT locomotive, a 4-wheeled petrol-driven Morris Cowley car engine and bonnet, mounted on a Decauville-type frame. This line did in fact run under the Rye and Camber Tramway and the bridge used was a loose brickwork style with a steel girder support.

The last passenger service ran in the summer of 1939. During all this time Mr Charles A. Gafford was associated with the Tramway, becoming Secretary early in 1900, and Managing Director soon afterwards and held this post until 1939.

Maps issued during the war years show an extension of about 100 yards beyond the end of the original line, but there is no record why this was put in. The Admiralty operated the line during World War II and this was used mainly for the transportation of armaments, the Rye to Golf Links section being used to move considerable materials (mainly wood) for the construction of the 1,000 ft-long Rother Pier and Jetty, the Admiralty laying a small branch from Golf Links station to the Jetty to take the material to the water's edge. They also concreted the section between Halfway House and Golf Links station thus linking to the Camber-Rye road, making the line a 'true' tramway, with track in the centre of the roadway.

After Dunkirk, a gap in the defences was identified between Dungeness and Rye. Lt Col Cantlie, who was in charge of rail-borne defence, wanted to lift one of the tracks of the double-line Romney, Hythe and Dymchurch Railway between Romney and Dungeness, and lay it across Walland Marsh to Camber; the tramway would have been re-gauged to 1 ft 3 in. and the RH&DR armoured train, which was equipped with anti-tank weapons, could have worked from Hythe to Rye. In the end this was not done.

At the end of hostilities, the area and tramway was handed back to the owners, but the line was in such a bad state of repair (with parts of the track missing and Camber station virtually demolished) that the company held a meeting and decided to wind-up the operation. In September 1947, the lease on the land was given back to Rye Corporation and parts of the track that were not cemented in, removed.

So ended the Rye and Camber Tramway.

A wet day at Rye terminus with the 4wP locomotive waiting with both coaches. Note the poor state of the buildings and platform when photographed on 11th April, 1931. *H.C. Casserley*

This view of *Camber* inside the locomotive shed at Rye in 1946 shows the dilapidated condition the disused Tramway had succumbed to. Note the spare set of wheels amidst all the rubbish.
Author's Collection

A wartime map of the area dated 1st June, 1941 (although of poor quality), shows gun and mine positions along the coast. The Rye and Camber Tramway is marked Steam Tramway and the Golf Links station is wrongly named Camber, the terminus at Camber Sands is named just 'Halt'!

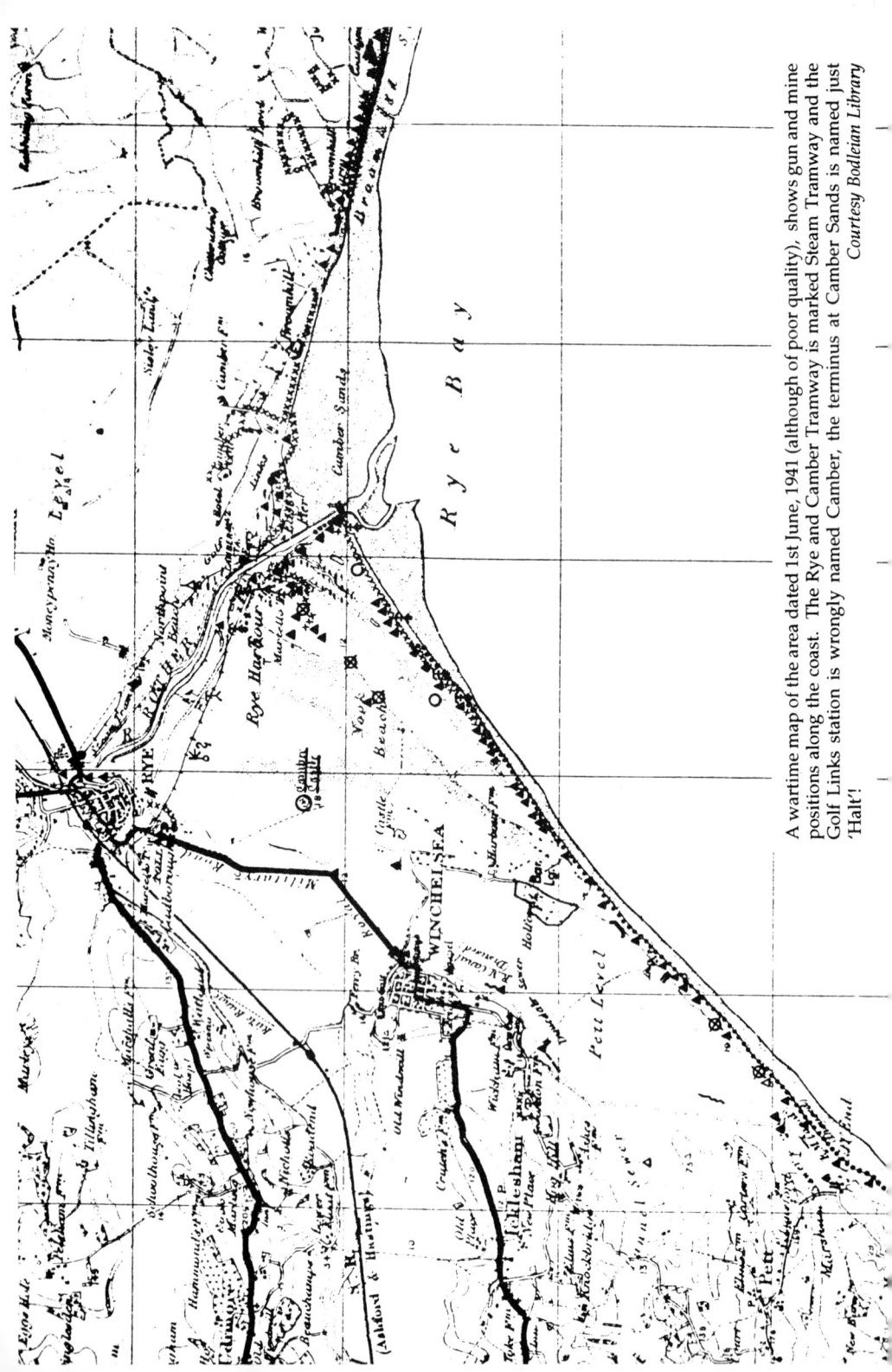

Courtesy Bodleian Library

The Scene Today

Fishing boats still land their catches by the Monkbretton Bridge near Rye, continuing an age old tradition probably dating back before the time of the Tramway, which had its terminus by the bridge.

Of the various buildings which made up the Tram station, there is no sign of any structure today and the footpath which now commences from the site, leads across lush green meadows with no trace of the route of the Tramway. A small pumping station now stands fairly close to where the original engine shed stood.

The first sign of the Tramway's existence is where the Broadwater Stream crosses its path as it flows into the River Rother. The Tramway crossed the stream on a small girder bridge and the two track bearing girders now serve to support a pipeline, whilst a short section of the embankment, on which the Tramway once ran, still remains; on the Rye side of the bridge.

From this bridge, the tramway crossed the Northpoint Beach which was worked extensively for the extraction of shingle by W.E. Colebrooke & Co., E.T. Jennings & Co. Ltd and lastly Amey Roadstone Corporation. This is now totally flooded (*see photograph*) and all signs of the Tramway have vanished. The lagoon so created is a Haven for the members of the Rye Windsurfers.

Beyond the North Beach, the Tramway passed Gorse Cottage, (which still stands) and Squatter's Right (which was demolished in 1983). Near to the site of the latter, a few wooden sleepers remain *in situ* to show the path the Tramway took.

The route now followed the course of the narrow concrete road to the Golf Links station and the Harbour Master's Office area. Indeed the course of the tramway can still been seen in this concreting; some on the outside of the rails in general (laid during the war) and some between the rails which was laid after the war. Rails are also visible near to the site of Squatter's Right and further along close to the 12th Tee of the Rye Golf Course. Golfers, in fact, drive across the old path of the Tramway from this tee.

Golf Links station is the only Tramway building now extant. The open platform awning has been filled in to give a pleasant windowed workroom. Formerly used by an artist (who left when a gale blew the roof off), the building is now used as a writing retreat by a local author. The interior has been painted white except for one or two wall panels which have been preserved with the writings of visitors to the Tramway going back to the 1930s. The exterior is painted green with white window frames.

The rails are still clearly visible in front of the station including part of the passing loop and the start of the spur (built by the Admiralty) which was laid for the construction of the Jetty.

Tramway rails were uncovered recently when an electricity cable was being laid from the Harbour Master's Office to a new navigational light about halfway along the jetty, close to where the Rother Jetty stood.

Close by here a ferry operated across the river to Rye Harbour and a series of concrete steps in the refurbished part of the Jetty mark the spot were it sailed from. Known locally as 'Ferry Steps', one can appreciate the hazards involved in crossing the river here by small ferry boat and one man rowing against a steady 5 knot current and the ebb and flow of the tide.

Where it all started! The site of the Rye terminus on 30th April, 1994, looking towards the sea. The route runs out behind the pumping station. *G. Gamble*

The Rye and Camber Tramway bridge over the Broadwater stream on 30th April, 1994, with a little of the embankment left on the Rye side. This bridge now carries pipes. Note the outskirts of Rye in the background. *G. Gamble*

Standing on the abutments of Broadwater bridge on 30th April, 1994 and looking towards the sea, the route of the Tramway is somewhat obscure (hence the drawn line showing approximately the route). The building in the distance is Gorse Cottage and the one on the right (marked with an arrow) Golf Links station, with the Harbour Master's Office on the extreme right.   *G. Gamble*

The track is still visible on 30th April, 1994 just past Gorse Cottage with the trackbed now concreted as a road.   *G. Gamble*

A close-up of the track work still *in situ* near to Gorse Cottage on 30th April, 1994. *G. Gamble*

Turning around and looking the other way from the position of the photographer in the lower view on the previous page (near the 12th Tee), the reader can see the Harbour Master's Office and just to the left of the mast, the top of Golf Links station. The cemented track can clearly be seen. *G. Gamble*

Golf Links station on 30th April, 1994, looking back towards Gorse Cottage. The station building is now being used as a retreat with the front platform canopy area having been enclosed. The platform remains so does the track, passing loop and even the branch to the Ferry steps. It is really amazing that after 50 years since trains ran, the rails and building are so well preserved.

G.Gamble

Golf Links station seen from the extension trackbed, looking towards Rye, March 1993.
John Miller

A view on 30th April, 1994, from the Harbour Master's Office with the crashed Dornier propeller (Do172) from World War II and various anchors adorning the grass. Golf Links station is off to the right and in the mid-distance can be seen Gorse Cottage. Ferry steps are by the mast of the boat and the short branch from Golf Links station ran to here.   *G. Gamble*

Looking from the new Ferry steps across the River Rother to Rye Harbour, with the lifeboat station in the middle centre. This is where the ferry row boat would have plied its trade from.
G. Gamble

The Harbour Master's Office commands a fine view out to sea with modern concrete walls holding back the water from the low land on the Camber side of the Rother. Inland the busy river leads one's eyes past Gorse Cottage on to the town of Rye situated on the hill in the background.

Across the river is Rye Harbour with some of its original cottages still standing and the Lifeboat station, soon to be modernised. The river has considerable use today by local and visiting pleasure boats and fishing boats. A display of old anchors is laid out in front of the Harbour Master's Office along with a bent propeller from a German Dornier Do172 which crashed in the estuary during World War II.

The path from Golf Links station to the Rye Golf Club is little used today as the modern golfer arrives by his own car along the busy road to Camber, which bisects the modern clubhouse and the professional's shop, attached to the 'Old Billy'. The much enlarged modern clubhouse has, within its walls, the vestiges of the small corrugated iron changing hut for golfers, which originally occupied the site.

From the Golf Links station, the path of the tramway is clearly marked by an embankment crossing what is now a part of the Golf Course. In one or two places the embankment has been levelled to allow access by golfers from the holes on one side to those on the other of the old Tramway. Approaching the site of Camber station, a golfers' shelter has recently been erected. From this point, the course of the Tramway is obscure and the shifting sands, plus the profusion of gorse bushes, seem to have covered over any small remains of the terminus station. The golf course now dominates the area and the sounds of happy day trippers on the Rye and Camber Tramway have long gone, being replaced by the frequent explosions from the military ranges at Lydd, whilst the noisy gulls scream overhead.

A bus service, operated by Stagecoach, now links Rye with Camber but there are many residents of both places who remember with true affection their carefree trips on the Rye and Camber Tramway.

A view from the trackbed (on a slight embankment) on 30th April, 1994, just past Golf Links station on the way to Camber Sands terminus. The route had turned through approximately 90 degrees and the reader can get a good idea of the area with, *on the left*, Rye Harbour (across the river), Harbour Master's Office, *right of centre*, and Gorse Cottage in the far distance *on the right*. *G. Gamble*

A view on 30th April, 1994 from Rye Harbour, on the other side of the River Rother, showing Golf Links station with the Golf Club behind in the far distance. *G. Gamble*

The Royal William Hotel *(right)* nicknamed 'The Old Billy' and the Professional's shop *(left)* at the Rye Golf Club site which once played such an important part in the life of the Rye and Camber Tramway. *G. Gamble*

The final straw that broke the Tramway; buses! Here the local Stagecoach bus service that now runs between Camber and Rye is seen crossing Monkbretton bridge on 30th April, 1994. Note the pumping station on the right that now stands on the old terminus site of Rye station. *G. Gamble*

Bibliography

Forgotten Railways: South East England by H.P. White, published by David and Charles
The Railway Magazine (Volume 31 and Volume 79)
Trains Illustrated (1972)
Narrow Gauge News (1965)
Rye Golf Club; The first 90 years by D. Vidler
Sussex Express: 1895, 1903 and 1908
The Colonel Stephens Railways by J. Scott-Morgan, published by David and Charles
The Rye and Camber Tramway by Peter Harding, published by the Author
Rye's Own Magazine, 1969
Meccano Magazine, 1924
The Engineer, 1927
Tenterden Terrier (K&ESR) Summer Edition 1976, *pp 20-22.*

Acknowledgements

The Public Record Office, Kew; The Bodleian Library, Oxford; the Newspaper Library, Colindale; Geoff Gamble and Roger Kidner. To all the photographers who dug deep from their collections.